DISCARDED

FROM FARM TO YOU

Sausage

Carol Jones

CHELSEA HOUSE
PUBLISHERS

A Haights Cross Communications Company

Philadelphia

Chelsea House Publishers
1974 Sproul Road, Suite 400
Broomall, PA 19008-0914

The Chelsea House world wide web address is www.chelseahouse.com

Library of Congress Cataloging-in-Publication Data Applied for.
ISBN 0-7910-7006-9

First published in 2002 by
MACMILLAN EDUCATION AUSTRALIA PTY LTD
627 Chapel Street, South Yarra, Australia, 3141

Edited by Anne McKenna
Text design by Judith Summerfeldt Grace
Cover design by Judith Summerfeldt Grace

Printed in China

Acknowledgements
The author wishes to thank Andrew and Theo Emmanouil of Andrew's Choice, and
Gottfried Schupfer of Don Smallgoods for their help with the writing of this book.

Cover photographs: Plate of wieners courtesy of Getty Images/Photodisc, sliced salami courtesy of Artville.

APL/Corbis © Roger Wood, p. 5, © Archivo Iconographico, p. 6, © Rykoff Collection, p. 7 (bottom), © Lake County Museum,
p. 7 (top), © Marc Garanger, pp. 8–9, © Owen Franken, p. 18, © Stuart Westmorland, p. 19 (right), © Ludovic Maisant, p. 28
(France), © Robert Holmes, p. 28 (Scotland), © Earl and Nazima Kowall, p. 29 (China); Artville, pp. 3 (top right), 29 (USA);
Coo-ee Picture Library, p. 19 (left); Copper Leife/Craig Forsythe, pp. 9 (top left), 20, 21 (top and bottom), 22 (top and
bottom), 24–26, 27 (left), [20–22 and 25–27 courtesy of Tibaldi Smallgoods], p. 28 (Israel), 29 (Australia); Getty Images/Image
Bank, p. 4, Photodisc, pp. 28–9 (map), 28 (Italy, Germany, and Spain), 29 (Austria); Imageaddict, pp. 16–17; Carol Jones,
pp. 3 (bottom left and right), 9 (top right), 10–15; Tibaldi Smallgoods, pp. 3 (top left), 27 (right).

Contents

The world of sausage

In many places in the world, unusual looking sausages hang in the windows of delicatessens.

The hanging sausages are dried or **cured** sausage. Fresh and cooked sausage is displayed in the refrigerator. Sausages are made from chopped or minced meat stuffed into a casing, or skin. These may be natural casings of animal **intestine**, **artificial** casings, or edible casings made from plant and animal material.

Sausage can be made from almost any kind of meat, but pork and beef are often used. It has flavorings added and often a **preservative** such as salt.

Sausage has been made for thousands of years throughout Europe, North Africa, the **Middle East** and China.

Children all around the world love sausages.

The history of sausage

Sausages are one of the earliest forms of cooked and **preserved** food.

Four thousand years ago, the Sumerians of southern Iraq were stuffing partly dried meat and spices into bags. These were not much like the sausages we know, but the idea was there. Around the same time in China, clever cooks were preserving meat in a similar way using many different recipes.

The ancient Greeks killed hogs in winter to make ham and bacon. They discovered that they could preserve the left-over bits by stuffing them into the animals' intestines with salt and spices. If they dried, smoked and hung them in a cool place, the meat would keep for months.

The ancient Greeks might have used this tool to make sausages.

Firsts

Almost 3,000 years ago, the Greek writer Homer was the first poet to mention sausages in his famous story of *The Odyssey*.

Sausages of many kinds were sold in the markets of ancient Rome. The word 'sausage' comes from the Latin word *salsus*, meaning salt. Latin was the language spoken by the Romans. Some of their recipes for sausage survive today. One popular smoked sausage called *lucanica* was made with pork, herbs and spices, peppercorns and pine nuts.

As the popularity of sausage grew, different kinds of sausage were often named after the places in which they were first made:

- Frankfurters came from Frankfurt in Germany.
- Wieners came from Vienna in Austria (the German name for Vienna is Wien).
- Polish sausage came from Poland.

An ancient Roman butcher

Strange but true!

In Ancient Rome, sausage was popular at banquets held by pagans (people who were neither Christian, Muslim nor Jewish). The Christian emperors thought everything pagan was bad so they banned sausage. For a while sausage was only available in secret.

The city of Frankfurt celebrated the 500th birthday of the frankfurter in 1987. However, it was the Americans who thought of putting the frankfurter in a roll, creating what we know today as the hot dog. These were first sold at a stand at Coney Island amusement park near New York in 1871.

Frankfurters

A 1946 advertisement for frankfurters, from the United States.

A Coney Island hot dog stand in the 1920s

Famous sausage

The name 'hot dog' was first used on a cold day in 1901. Harry Stevens was losing money on his ice cream stand at the New York Polo Grounds. He bought up all the thin sausages, then called dachshunds (German dogs with a long, low body), and rolls he could find, yelling out, 'They're red hot! Get your dachshund sausages while they're red hot!' The local newspaper cartoonist drew a picture of the event. But because he couldn't spell 'dachshund' he changed it to 'hot dog'!

Kinds of sausage

There are three main kinds of sausage: fresh, cooked and dried.

1. Fresh sausages

Fresh sausages can be made from many kinds of meat. Pork, beef, lamb or veal are often used, but they can also be made from **game** or poultry. Fresh sausages usually include salt to help bind the meat, spices, herbs and often **cereal**. They can be kept for two or three days in the refrigerator and are fried, grilled or boiled for eating.

2. Cooked sausages

Many cooked sausages are smoked by cooking them in an oven with the smoke from **smoldering** sawdust. They will keep from a few days to a few weeks in the refrigerator. Cooked sausages such as frankfurters and blood sausage can be reheated before eating. Others such as Polish sausage and mortadella are eaten cold.

In Germany there are 1,500 different varieties of sausage.

3. Dried sausages

For dried sausages, the meat is usually uncooked. Instead it is cured by the salt and spices. This kills any harmful germs. Then it is hung in a cool, dry place where the air can **circulate**. Dried sausages such as Italian salami or Chinese lap cheong will keep for several months in a cool, dry place if left whole. They are usually eaten cold.

Dried sausages and other meats hanging in an Italian delicatessen

Fresh sausages are a favorite food for cooking on the grill.

Preservation

Smoking is an ancient way of preserving food. The substances given off in the smoke fumes destroy germs that would usually make the food go bad.

How sausages are made

Although sausages are often made in large factories, many small butchers also make them. Some sell the sausages only from their shops. Others sell them to delicatessens and restaurants.

The butchers shown here are making smoked cheese kranskies — a German-style sausage.

The sausages are being filled by hand.

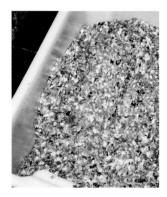

Pork and beef meat

The smoking oven has electric heating elements. The sawdust used to cook these sausages smolders in a drawer underneath.

Sausages hanging in the smoking oven

Ingredients

To make these sausages, the following ingredients are used:

- pork and beef meat
- salt
- spices
- vintage cheddar cheese
- natural casings made from pig intestines.

Lamb casings are small and used for sausages such as chipolatas. Beef casings are used for large cooked sausages such as mortadella. China exports more natural casings than any other country.

Tools and equipment

Most of the tools used by the butchers are similar to those used for centuries, except they are now powered by electricity. Once they would have been powered by hand or fire. Some of the tools used are:

- a computerized smoking oven
- a mincer
- a sausage filler
- tubs for mixing
- sharp knives.

Method

Preparing the ingredients

The afternoon before making cheese kranskies, the butcher cuts the meat into large cubes. He uses a mixture of pork and beef. The cheese is cut into cubes and the correct amounts of spices are measured out.

Mincing the meat

The meat is put through the mincer to grind it finely. Then it is salted and placed in the refrigerator to cure overnight. As well as acting as a preservative, the salt helps bind the minced meat together. The salt makes the meat turn pink, like ham.

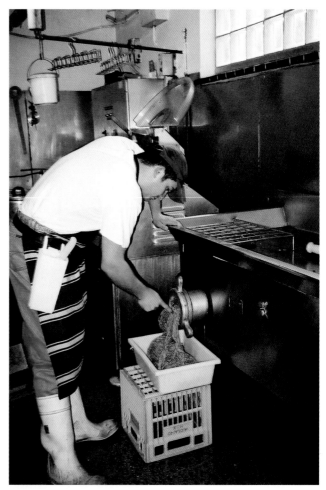

Mincing the meats

Adding the salt

Mixing the ingredients

The next morning, the spices and cubes of cheese are added to the prepared meat in a large tub. Some butchers add cereal to their sausages for extra bulk but these butchers use only meat. If they were making fresh sausages they would use herbs instead of spices.

Filling the casings

The butchers use natural casings made from pig intestines. The casings are placed over a hollow rod on the sausage filler. The meat mixture is forced through the rod into the casings. The butcher works quickly to keep up with the machine. When filled, the casing looks like one very long sausage.

Filling the casing

Linking the sausage

The butcher now makes the individual sausages. He twists the filled sausage casing to form links where the sausages can later be cut. This makes a long line of sausages.

Making the links in the sausage

Preparing the sawdust

The butcher measures the sawdust for the smoking oven. A mixture of fine and coarse sawdust from hardwood and oregon timber is used. Vine leaves or fruitwood sawdust could also be used and would give a different flavor to the sausages.

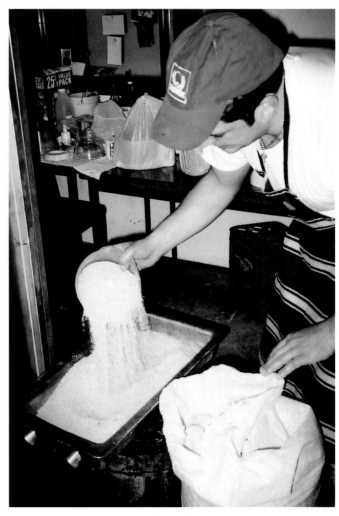

Measuring the sawdust for the smoking oven

Smoking and cooking the sausages

The smoking oven can hold 200 sausages hung on stainless steel rods. Its temperature is controlled by a computer. The sausages are cooked until a computerized **probe** senses that the inside temperature of the sausages has reached about 160 degrees Fahrenheit (70 degrees Celsius). This takes about two-and-one-half hours.

While they are cooking, air is circulated over the sawdust. The sawdust needs just enough air to smolder, but not so much that it will catch fire.

Once the sausages are cooked they are hung in the butchers' refrigerated room ready for sale.

The sausages hang in the smoking oven.

The sausage factory

Most of the sausages we buy are made in large factories. Pork is often used in sausages.

From farm to consumer

Follow the flowchart to see how hogs are raised and how pork is **processed** and made into frankfurters at a large **meat-packing plant**. It is then transported to stores for sale to the **consumer**.

Read more about each stage of the sausage-making process and how sausages are marketed and sold on pages 18 to 27. Look for the flowchart symbols that represent each stage of the process.

Raising hogs
Pork meat for sausages comes from hogs. Hogs are raised on hog farms.

Packaging the sausages
Packaging materials may be made elsewhere and delivered to the factory. Sausages may be packaged in bulk or **vacuum-packed** in plastic.

Transport and storage
The finished sausages are loaded onto **pallets** and transported to stores or ports.

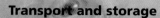

Transport and storage

When the hogs are ready to be killed, they are transported from the hog farm to the meat-packing plant in trucks.

Processing the meat

At the meat-packing plant, the hogs are killed and their meat is prepared for making sausages.

Manufacturing the sausages

Next, the pork meat is minced and fed into casings to form sausages.

Transport and storage

Pig **carcasses** are stored in refrigerated rooms.

Marketing and selling sausages

Sausages can be sold locally in butcher's shops, delicatessens and supermarkets, or exported to other countries.

Buying sausages

The consumer stores fresh and cooked sausages in the refrigerator. Uncut dried sausage can be kept in a cupboard.

Raising hogs

One of the most common meats used in sausage is pork. Hogs are raised on farms.

Some farmers let their hogs graze outside but most hogs live in large sheds. They are fed a special diet of grains so that their meat will not be too fatty. Some sheds hold more than 20,000 female hogs called sows.

The sheds are kept very clean and the temperature is controlled so that the hogs are healthy.

A large hog shed

Transport and storage

Hog farmers sell their hogs to meat-packing plants. The hogs are transported to the plant in livestock trucks and kept in pens until ready to be killed.

Types of hogs

Popular breeds of hog are the Chester White, Landrace, Berkshire and Duroc. Each sow will have two litters a year, usually of about ten live piglets. Piglets grow quickly and are usually sent to the meat-packing plant when they weigh about 130 to 160 pounds (60 to 80 kilograms).

Piglets may be **weaned** from their mothers between two and eight weeks.

Vietnamese Pot-bellied pigs

Hog farm workers

Farmers

Farm hands

Drivers

Processing the meat

Meat is processed at meat-packing plants. Each country has laws about how animals are to be killed without pain. The hogs are made unconscious by gas or electricity before they are killed so that they suffer as little as possible.

The carcass is then soaked in hot water to loosen hairs, then tumbled in a dehairing machine. It is hung and sent through gas burners to burn off the last hairs. After washing, the carcass is cut in half and hung in a refrigerated room to cool.

Meat-packing plant workers
Slaughterers
Transport workers

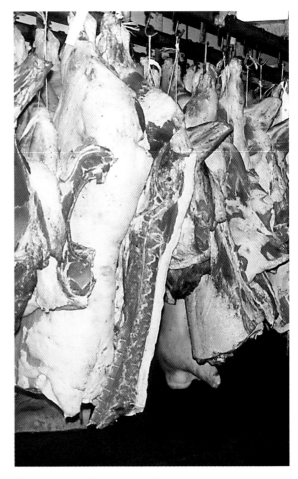

Carcasses hanging in a refrigerated room

Transport and storage

Carcasses are stored in refrigerated rooms. Carcasses to be exported are frozen, then shipped.

Boning the meat

A meat inspector inspects the carcasses to make sure they are fit for humans to eat.

The meat intended for making sausages goes to a boning room. There the meat is cut from the bone and placed in large crates.

The boned meat is placed in large plastic crates.

Boning the meat

Strange but true!

Almost every part of the hog can be used. Organs are sold as **offal**. Blood can be made into a sausage called blood sausage. Bones are crushed and used as fertilizer. Intestines are used to make sausage casings. Fats can be boiled down to make tallow for candles and soap. Skins can be tanned for leather. Bristles can be used in brushes.

Manufacturing the sausages

Meat-packing factories use machinery costing many millions of dollars. This is how a frankfurter is made.

Fresh or frozen pork and beef are fed into a gigantic mincer and chopper and minced through a metal plate with very small holes. Mincers that chop frozen meat are extremely powerful. The minced meat moves by **conveyor belt** to a ribbon mixer, which can hold about 3,500 pounds (1,600 kilograms). Other ingredients are added here, such as icy water, salt, spices and soy **protein**. Two ribbons of stainless steel turn in opposite directions to mix the ingredients.

The mincer at work

Minced meat moving along a conveyor belt

Transport and storage

Crates of meat arriving from the boning room are moved by forklift for weighing and checking. They are stored overnight in refrigerated rooms for the next day's production.

Filling the casings

Next the meat is fed into a machine that cuts the mixture up even more, and then into trolleys to be moved to the filling machine.

A hoist empties the trolleys into a hopper, which feeds mixture into the filling machine. The mixture is pushed at high speed through a filling horn into artificial sausage casings. The machine has a twisting head that makes the links in the sausages.

Sausages are filled and placed on racks.

Manufacturing workers

Food technologists

Chemists

Engineers

Production-line workers

Transport workers

Additives

As well as meat, salt and spices, frankfurters may contain:
- artificial colorings and flavorings
- shelf-life improvers to keep the sausages fresh for longer
- **emulsifiers** to make the mixture smoother.

There are government rules stating how much meat sausages must contain.

The sausage mixture moves through the plant on conveyor belts and overhead rails.

Cooking the sausages

Racks of sausages are cooked in ovens the size of rooms. Here, the sausages are first dried, then smoked, then cooked. Sawdust from hardwood timber is used for smoking. This gives the frankfurters added color and flavor. After cooking, the sausages need to be chilled as quickly as possible. The racks move from the ovens to a **brine** chiller. This is a large room where sausages are sprayed with cold brine to lower their temperature.

If the frankfurters are made with artificial casings, which cannot be eaten, they are fed into an automatic peeler. A knife makes a tiny slit in the casing and steam is used to remove it. Natural casings are not removed because they can be eaten.

Frankfurters have added color and flavor because they are smoked.

 Transport and storage

After packaging, sausages are loaded onto pallets and moved to refrigerated rooms to await transport.

Packaging the sausages

Sausages may be packaged in bulk or vacuum-packed in plastic for sale in supermarkets and other stores.

The links of sausage are carried on a conveyor belt to the packaging area. Some are packed in plastic-lined boxes for delivery to delicatessens and large customers such as fast-food outlets. Sausages for small shops and supermarkets are vacuum-packed so that they stay fresh longer.

The **manufacturer's** brand design and a list of ingredients are printed on the packaging.

The packaged sausages are loaded onto pallets and moved by forklift.

Packaging workers

Engineers

Production-line workers

Graphic designers

Transport workers

Forklift drivers

The pallets are transported by truck to shops and supermarkets or to large customers such as fast-food outlets.

Marketing and selling sausages

Sausages can be sold locally or exported to other countries. Meat-packing plants use advertising to encourage consumers to buy their product.

Workers from meat-packing plants called merchandisers visit stores to make sure that they are receiving the kinds and amounts of sausages and meat products they need. They also organize special displays and tastings to help advertise their company's products.

Meat-packing companies can also afford to advertise their products to a larger audience. They might place ads in magazines or on television. Some companies have their own websites to tell consumers about their products.

A range of sausages for sale in a delicatessen

Home storage

Fresh and cooked sausage must be kept in the refrigerator. Fresh sausages will keep for a few days. Some cooked sausages will keep longer if left uncut. Dried sausages will keep in a cool, dry cupboard for several weeks if uncut. Once cut, they should be wrapped in plastic wrap and used within five days.

Marketing and sales workers

Merchandisers

Shelf-fillers

Checkout operators

Shop assistants

Butchers

Graphic designers

Copywriters

Buying sausages

Meat-packing plants package their product in different ways to suit different consumers. For example, large dried or cooked sausages are sold in delicatessens where the shop assistant slices the sausage for the consumer as needed. Smaller sausages are bought whole. Sometimes dried or cooked sausages are sold sliced and vacuum-packed for sale in supermarkets.

Fresh sausages are bought in butchers' shops. They are weighed to meet the consumer's needs. The consumer can choose from a huge variety of fresh, cooked and dried sausages. They can be eaten boiled, grilled, fried or cold, in a bread roll, with salad or vegetables, or simply on their own.

A butcher weighs some sausages.

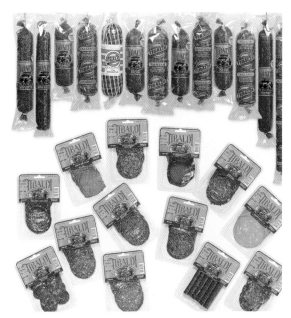

Sausages can be packaged whole or in slices.

Sausages around the world

There are about 1,500 different kinds of sausage in Germany.

In Poland kransky is a popular sausage.

The Scottish dish haggis could be called a sausage. It is made from sheep's offal and oatmeal boiled in the sheep's stomach.

Spain is famous for its chorizo, a very spicy sausage made from pork and red peppers.

Sausages from Israel are usually made of lamb because Jewish people do not eat pork.

France is famous for its sausages. They are an important part of French charcuterie, or cured meats. They include Lyons sausage, cervelat (saveloy) and blood sausage (above).

Italy is the home of the dried and cured sausage called salami. Mortadella is a popular large smoked sausage from Italy.

Austria is the home of the wiener, a smoke-cooked sausage like a frankfurter.

In the United States, people eat about 20 billion hot dogs a year!

Lap cheong is a wind-dried sausage from China, usually made from pork and pork fat. Sometimes the pork is mixed with duck liver. The sausages are tied together with string and sold in pairs.

Australians love sausages cooked on a grill.

Make your own meat patties

Use this recipe to make delicious meat patties at home with help from an adult.

Meat patties

Ingredients

- ○ 1 large onion
- ○ 1 tablespoon of chopped parsley
- ○ $2\frac{1}{4}$ pounds of finely minced pork
- ○ 1 tablespoon of salt
- ○ 1 teaspoon of white pepper
- ○ pinch of nutmeg

Equipment

- ○ sharp knife
- ○ chopping board
- ○ large bowl
- ○ frying pan or grill

Method

1. Wash your hands carefully and make sure all equipment is very clean.
2. Ask an adult to help you chop the onion and parsley finely.
3. Place the minced pork in a large bowl and add the other ingredients. Mix thoroughly with your hands.
4. Wet your hands, take a handful of the mixture and roll it into a ball. Make the remaining mixture into balls. Squash the balls flat.
5. Cook the patties by frying or grilling.

Glossary

additives   substances added to improve something

artificial   made by people

brine   salt water

carcasses   dead bodies of animals

cereal   grain

circulate   go around

consumer   person who buys goods or services

conveyor belt   an endless strip of material, such as rubber, on rollers used to move something

cured   preserved by salting or drying

emulsifiers   salts that help one substance blend with another

food technologists   workers who scientifically test or treat food

game   wild animals or birds kept for food

intestine   part of the body that helps digest food

manufacturers   people or companies that make goods

meat-packing plant   a place where animals are killed for their meat

Middle East   area around eastern Mediterranean Sea, from Turkey to North Africa

offal   inside parts of an animal that can be eaten

pallets   large trays

preservative   ingredient to keep food fresh

preserved   kept fresh for a long time

probe   something that tests

processed   treated in a special way

protein   body-building chemical substance

smoldering   burning without a flame

vacuum-packed   tightly wrapped in plastic so the air cannot get in

weaned   replaced mother's milk with other food

Index